TIMELINE HISTORY

SPORTS

From Ancient Olympics to the Super Bowl

Liz Miles

Heinemann Library
Chicago, Illinois

Edited by Louise Galpine and Diyan Leake
Designed by Richard Parker
Original illustrations © Capstone Global Library Ltd 2011
Illustrated by Jeff Edwards
Picture research by Hannah Taylor

Originated by Capstone Global Library Ltd
Printed in the United States of America in North Mankato, Minnesota.   062015   009003RP

17 16 15
10 9 8 7 6 5 4

Library of Congress Cataloging-in-Publication Data
Miles, Liz.
  Sports : from ancient Olympics to the Super Bowl / Liz Miles.
     p. cm. -- (Timeline history)
  Includes bibliographical references and index.
  ISBN 978-1-4329-3805-5 (hc) -- ISBN 978-1-4329-3813-0
(pb) 1. Sports--History--Juvenile literature. I. Title.
  GV571.M525 2011
  796.09--dc22
                        2009048963

Acknowledgments
The author and publisher are grateful to the following for permission to reproduce copyright material: Alamy Images pp. **10** top (© Lordprice Collection), **12** top (© Imagepast), **26** (© NearTheCoast.com); Bishop Museum Archive p. **13**; Corbis pp. **7** top (Amit Dey), **8** (Atlantide Phototravel), **16** bottom (Bettmann), **18** top (Bettmann), **20** bottom (Xinhua Press/Zhang Yanhui), **22** top (Bettmann), **22** bottom (Leo Mason), **25** (epa/Kerim Okten); Getty Images pp. **5** (AFP Photo/Fabrice Coffrini), **10** bottom (AFP Photo/Luis Acosta), **12** bottom (The Bridgeman Art Library), **14** (Transcendental Graphics/Mark Rucker), **15** bottom (Popperfoto), **16** top (Diamond Images/Kidwiler Collection), **17**, **18** bottom (Hulton Archive), **19** (Diamond Images/Kidwiler Collection), **20** top (Popperfoto), **21** Express/Clive Limpkin), **24** bottom (AFP Photo/Joe Klamar), **27** (Jasper Juinen); Motoring Picture Library p. **15** top; Photolibrary pp. **6** (Walter Bibikow), **7** bottom (View Stock), **11** (North Wind Pictures); Rex Features p. **24** top (KPA/Zuma); The Advertising Archives p. **23**; The Art Archive pp. **4** (Dagli Orti), **9** top, **9** bottom (Dagli Orti).

Cover photograph of Reggie Bush #25 of the New Orleans Saints running with the ball against Clint Session #55 of the Indianapolis Colts during Super Bowl XLIV on February 7, 2010 at Sun Life Stadium in Miami Gardens, Florida, reproduced with permission of Getty Images (Jonathan Daniel).

Every effort has been made to contact copyright holders of material reproduced in this book. Any omissions will be rectified in subsequent printings if notice is given to the publisher.

Contents

Historical time is divided into two major periods. BCE is short for "Before the Common Era"—that is, the time before the Christian religion began. This is the time up to the year 1 BCE. CE is short for "Common Era." This means the time from the year 1 BCE to the present. For example, when a date is given as 1000 CE, it is 1,000 years after the year 1 BCE. The abbreviation *c.* stands for *circa*, which is Latin for "around."

Any words appearing in the text in bold, **like this**, are explained in the glossary.

The Sports Buzz

People enjoy sports for many different reasons: to get fit, compete, break records, feel part of a team, and make money. Some people play just for fun!

Ever-changing

Sports themselves have changed a lot through time. Gradually new sports appeared and the first rules were made. We will see how sports grew to be a common way for people to have fun—as well as to make money. Other developments have influenced sports. New technology has provided better equipment, such as rackets and balls. International competitions only became possible when transportation improved. When there were no aircraft or fast boats, athletes could not travel overseas. Now spectators jet all over the world to see competitions.

Determined

Over the centuries, one thing has not changed—to be successful in sports, people must practice often, and hard! Throughout history, people have worked hard to stand out from the crowd as sports stars. Determined to win, they give most of their time to their sport.

Pictures from ancient tombs show that about 4,000 years ago ordinary Egyptians played many of the sports we enjoy today, from wrestling to high jumps.

Jamaican sprinter Usain Bolt broke world records at the 2009 World Athletics Championships in Berlin, Germany.

Timelines

The information in this book is on a timeline. A timeline shows you events from history in the order they happened. The big timeline in the middle of each page gives you details of a certain time in history (see below).

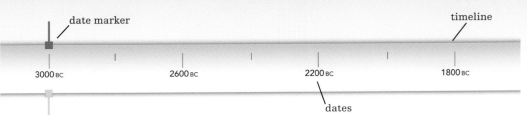

date marker

timeline

3000 BC   2600 BC   2200 BC   1800 BC

dates

Some dates are exact. For example, the first modern Olympic Games were held in 1896. Others are more general because there were no written records of an event or it took place over a period of time. The smaller timeline at the bottom of each page shows you how the page you are reading fits into history as a whole. You will read about sports from all around the world. Each entry on the main timeline is in a different color. This color shows you which continent the information is about. The map below shows you how this color coding works. Pale green indicates events that took place on more than one continent or worldwide.

North America

Europe

Asia

Africa

South America

Australia and Oceania

Worldwide

Ancient Sports

In **prehistoric** times, people spent most of their time hunting for food. But they may have enjoyed the thrill of running and swimming, too. The oldest evidence of sports comes from the first **civilizations**, such as those of the ancient Greeks and Egyptians.

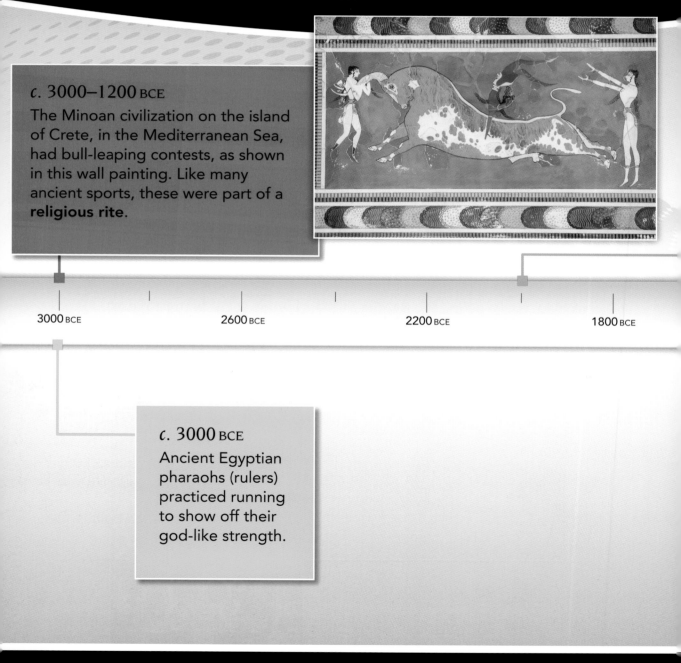

c. 3000–1200 BCE

The Minoan civilization on the island of Crete, in the Mediterranean Sea, had bull-leaping contests, as shown in this wall painting. Like many ancient sports, these were part of a **religious rite**.

3000 BCE   2600 BCE   2200 BCE   1800 BCE

c. 3000 BCE

Ancient Egyptian pharaohs (rulers) practiced running to show off their god-like strength.

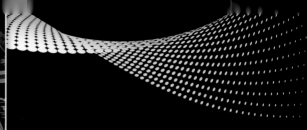

c. 2000 BCE

Kabaddi was first played in India. It is like a mix of wrestling and **rugby** in which players make raids on the other team while holding their breath.

600 BCE

Persian soldiers played the first recorded game of polo. They played on horseback with a stick and a ball. Some say the ball was the head of an enemy soldier.

1400 BCE	1000 BCE	600 BCE

776 BCE   ANCIENT OLYMPICS

The first ancient Olympic Games were held in Olympia, Greece, in honor of the Greek god Zeus. The first Olympics had one event—a men's sprint of nearly 200 meters (219 yards), as painted on this vase. Later, it included the discus, javelin, and weight-lifting. The women had separate games in honor of the goddess Hera.

Deadly Sports

As populations grew in cities in Europe and Asia, bigger crowds gathered to watch sports. Dangerous sports were very popular. People began to bet money on who might win. Prizes, such as cash, were often given to the winning athletes.

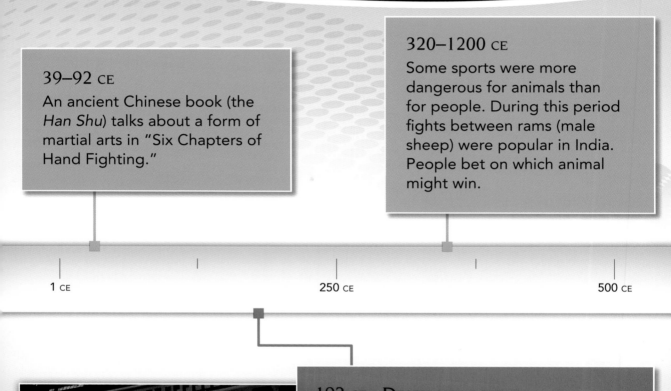

39–92 CE

An ancient Chinese book (the *Han Shu*) talks about a form of martial arts in "Six Chapters of Hand Fighting."

320–1200 CE

Some sports were more dangerous for animals than for people. During this period fights between rams (male sheep) were popular in India. People bet on which animal might win.

1 CE   250 CE   500 CE

192 CE   DEATH AND DEFEAT

Chariot racing was at its most popular in ancient Rome. Up to 250,000 people watched in the huge Circus Maximus arena. In a crash, charioteers often got caught in the horses' reins and were dragged along the ground. They often died. Many charioteers were **slaves** who hoped to win enough money to buy their freedom.

1185–1233

Fearsome Japanese fighters called samurai practiced sword fighting, horse-riding, and archery. They believed that it was better to die than be defeated.

750 CE   1000 CE   1250 CE

1100s CE

In Britain and France, knights practiced their fighting skills in jousting tournaments.

present day

Early Ball Games

All kinds of ball games were played around the world. They were without rules and often dangerous. The balls were made from any materials that were available. Rubber plants that could make bouncing balls only grew in certain parts of the world.

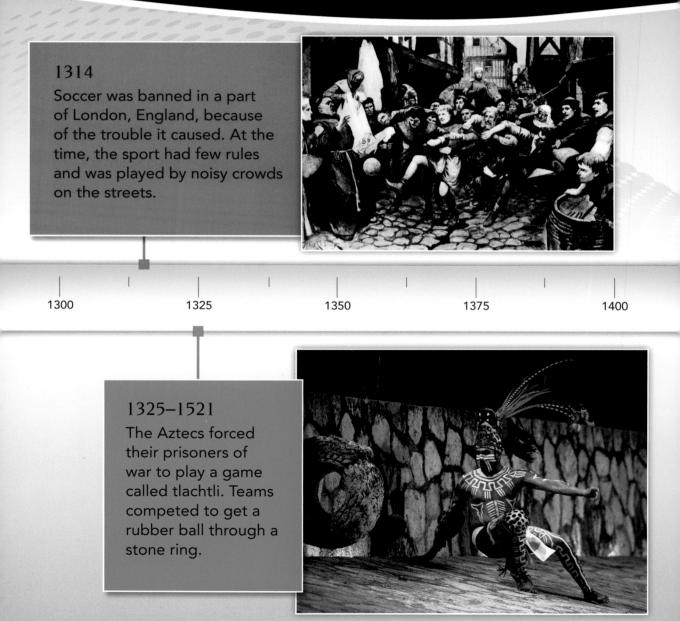

1314

Soccer was banned in a part of London, England, because of the trouble it caused. At the time, the sport had few rules and was played by noisy crowds on the streets.

1300   1325   1350   1375   1400

1325–1521

The Aztecs forced their prisoners of war to play a game called tlachtli. Teams competed to get a rubber ball through a stone ring.

1400s

Golf began to be played in Scotland. Players hit their feather-filled ball into a series of holes over hilly land.

1492

When Christopher Columbus landed in the West Indies, he witnessed the Tainos people playing a two-team game on a clay court called a batey. A rubber ball had to be kept in the air by hitting it with any part of the body except the hands.

1425   1450   1475   1500

1400s NATIVE AMERICAN GAMES

Many Native American peoples played stick and ball games similar to today's **lacrosse**. The Iroquois played baggataway. They used a single stick with a triangular net to throw and catch a ball made of bone or rock.

present day

Rules and Regulations

By the 1500s, some sports became less rough in the West. Rules were agreed upon. By 1800 there were many slow-paced sports, like **cricket**, billiards (which is like pool), and bowls (a kind of lawn bowling). In the East, sports were often linked to ceremonies or were only for the rich.

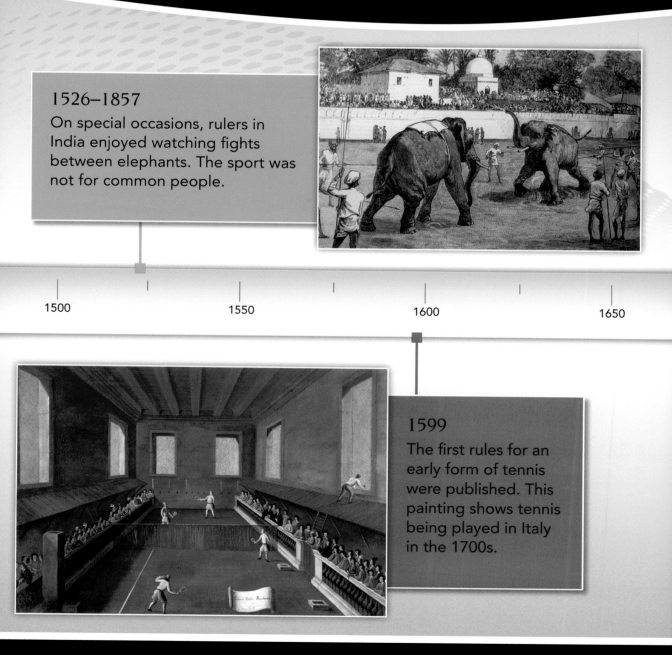

1526–1857

On special occasions, rulers in India enjoyed watching fights between elephants. The sport was not for common people.

1500	1550	1600	1650

1599

The first rules for an early form of tennis were published. This painting shows tennis being played in Italy in the 1700s.

c. 1700

A popular form of **kung fu** developed in China, called wing chun (which means "eternal springtime"). A legend says that it is named after a woman who used this style of fighting to beat a warlord.

1744

Rules for cricket were written down. Some gentlemen in London felt it was impossible to play cricket fairly without any common rules. Their first "Laws of Cricket" still form the basis of cricket today.

1700   1750   1800

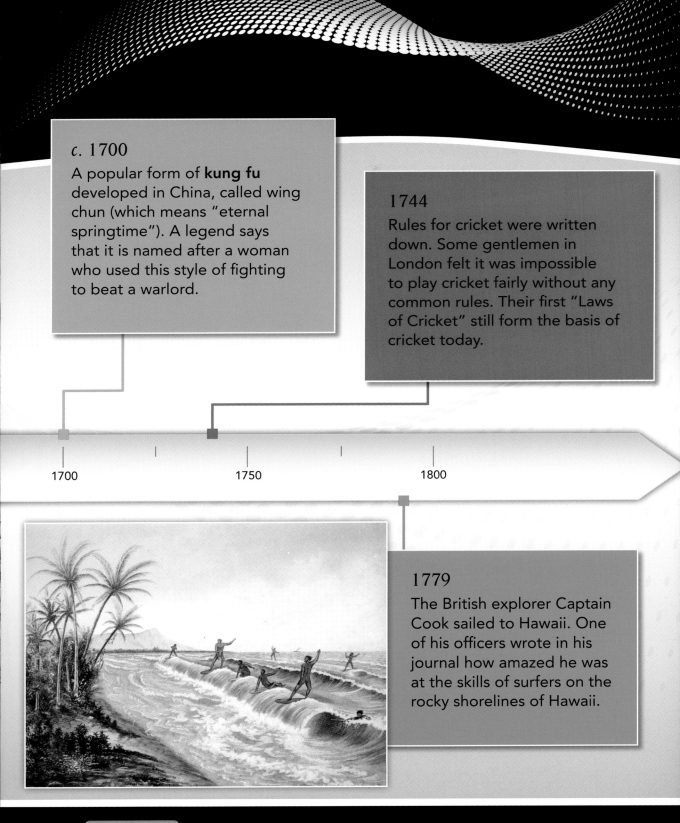

1779

The British explorer Captain Cook sailed to Hawaii. One of his officers wrote in his journal how amazed he was at the skills of surfers on the rocky shorelines of Hawaii.

A Changing World

By the 1800s, the effects of the **Industrial Revolution** changed the world of sports. Improved transportation, such as steamships and steam trains, led to the first county, national, and world championships. Growing populations in cities turned to sports for fun. Motor racing was made possible by the invention of the **engine**.

1845

The first U.S. baseball teams and clubs formed in towns and cities. In 1869 the first **professional** team was formed: the Cincinnati Red Stockings (right).

1840   1850   1860   1870

1876

The rules of badminton were written down, based on how the game was played in Poona, India. Badminton clubs began to form in the United States and Europe.

1877

The English **cricket** team traveled by steamboat to Melbourne, Australia, for the first cricket Test match. Australia won by 45 runs.

1883

The first **rugby** Home Nations Championship was held. It is said that rugby was invented when a soccer player at the Rugby School in Warwickshire, England, picked up the ball and ran with it. In the United States, football soon grew out of a mix of rugby and soccer.

1895

The first organized motor race took place on roads in France.

1880 — 1890 — 1900

1896

Crowds and athletes traveled to the first modern Olympic Games. They were held in Athens, Greece.

Prejudice in Sports

By the 1920s female athletes proved that they had the strength and skill to do what had been "men-only" sports. However, Africans and African Americans were still excluded because of **racial prejudice**.

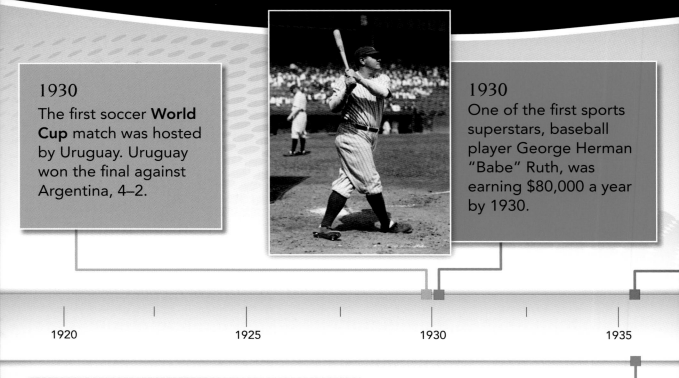

1930

The first soccer **World Cup** match was hosted by Uruguay. Uruguay won the final against Argentina, 4–2.

1930

One of the first sports superstars, baseball player George Herman "Babe" Ruth, was earning $80,000 a year by 1930.

1920   1925   1930   1935

1936

African Americans Louise Stokes (back row, third from left) and Tidye Pickett (back row, first on right) were finally allowed to compete as relay runners in the Olympic Games. In 1932 racial prejudice had caused them to be excluded from the games.

1936

Hitler's Nazi Germany hosted the Olympic Games in Berlin. Hitler believed that only white-skinned, blue-eyed, fair-haired people could do well in sports. He was proved wrong when African-American athlete Jesse Owens won four gold medals at the games.

1940   1945   1950

1940s SEGREGATION

Around the world, **segregation** in sports was still common. In the United States, African-American athletes were usually only allowed to enter "black-only" sports events or teams. In 1947 Jackie Robinson became the first African-American baseball player to play in modern Major League Baseball.

Sports on the Screen

The invention of television allowed more people to watch sports. It also brought **advertising** and **sponsorship**, which allowed sports teams and organizations to raise money. Athletes could make a living with their skills.

1950s
Basketball player Bob Cousy (wearing number 14, right) was in great demand and insisted on a huge salary before agreeing to play for the Boston Celtics.

1950   1951   1952   1953   1954

1953
U.S. golfer Arnold Palmer gained a big salary from prizes and advertising. Here he poses for a sports equipment advertisement.

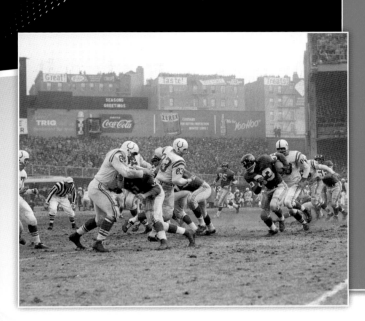

1958 TELEVISION SPORTS

About 45 million viewers watched the nail-biting National Football League (NFL) Championship Game on television. The Baltimore Colts defeated the New York Giants 23–17 during overtime. The NFL Championship Game was the first **professional** football game to draw a big television audience. The Colts–Giants game became known as "the Greatest Game Ever Played" and made the sport very popular.

1955   1956   1957   1958

1954

British athlete Roger Bannister was the first to run a mile in under four minutes.

1956

At the Australian Olympics, a match between the Hungary and **USSR** water polo teams became violent. A month earlier the USSR had invaded Hungary.

Sports for Everyone

Desegregation in public schools and public organizations in the United States began to take place in 1954. Protests against continuing racism in sports and **apartheid** in South Africa grew. Soon many more Africans began to win championships. The Paralympics allowed people with disabilities to compete internationally.

1960

The Ethiopian runner Abebe Bikila was the winner of the Olympic marathon. As a last-minute replacement for a teammate, Bikila had no comfortable shoes— so he ran barefoot.

| 1960 | 1961 | 1962 | 1963 | 1964 |

1960   PARALYMPICS

The first Paralympic Games were held in Rome, Italy. They involved 400 athletes with **spinal cord** injuries. The athletes competed in eight sports, including fencing, field events, and table tennis. Today, people with all kinds of disabilities compete in the Paralympics. South African sprinter Oscar Pritorius won gold in the 2008 Paralympics (right).

1965

The American League All-Star baseball game was to be played in the city of New Orleans, Louisiana. But when African-American players were turned away from some restaurants, the players protested. The event was moved to another city—Houston, Texas.

| 1965 | 1966 | 1967 | 1968 |

1965

The first Pan-African Games (now called the All-Africa Games) were held in Congo. People in many countries were united against apartheid. Anti-apartheid protestors (right) demonstrated when white South African **cricket** players came to London.

Money earned from prizes and sponsors turned **amateur** champions into **professional** sports stars. Some greedy athletes broke the rules and took drugs to help them win. But most just practiced hard.

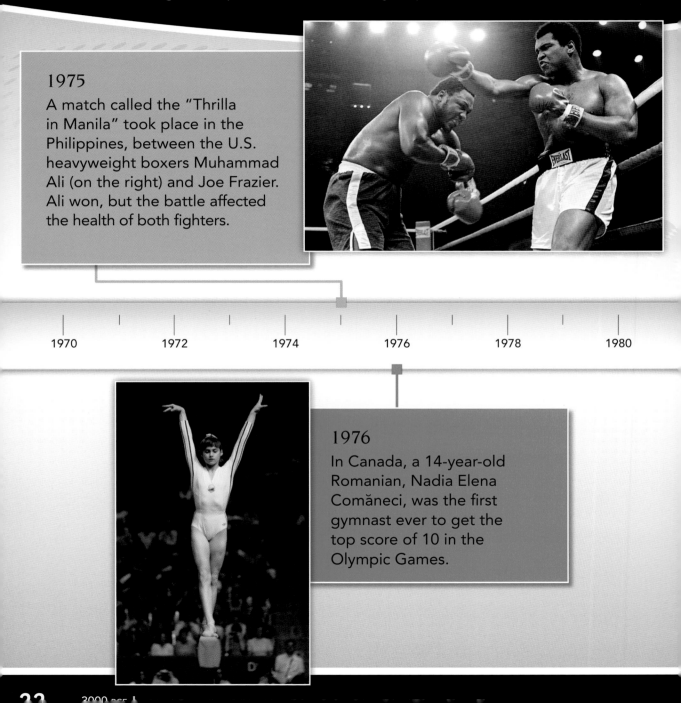

1975

A match called the "Thrilla in Manila" took place in the Philippines, between the U.S. heavyweight boxers Muhammad Ali (on the right) and Joe Frazier. Ali won, but the battle affected the health of both fighters.

1970   1972   1974   1976   1978   1980

1976

In Canada, a 14-year-old Romanian, Nadia Elena Comăneci, was the first gymnast ever to get the top score of 10 in the Olympic Games.

MICHAEL JORDAN 1
ISAAC NEWTON   0

NIKE AIR

1985

U.S. basketball superstar Michael Jordan received $2.5 million from sportswear company Nike, so that Nike could use Jordan's name and image to make a new line of sneakers called Air Jordans.

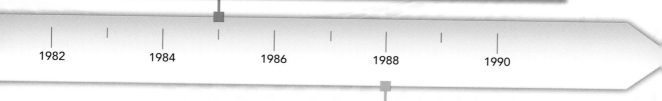

| 1982 | 1984 | 1986 | 1988 | 1990 |

1988   DOPING

Canadian sprinter Ben Johnson was found guilty of taking drugs at the Olympics in Seoul, South Korea, and his gold medal was taken away. Other sports stars took drugs to make them perform better. This is called "doping." Scientists found new ways to test athletes for these drugs.

Extreme Sports

Sports have become bigger and faster, and they attract enormous sums of money. New and dangerous sports, known as extreme sports, have been developed. New drugs have been invented that enhance an athlete's performance. Banned drugs are becoming harder to detect.

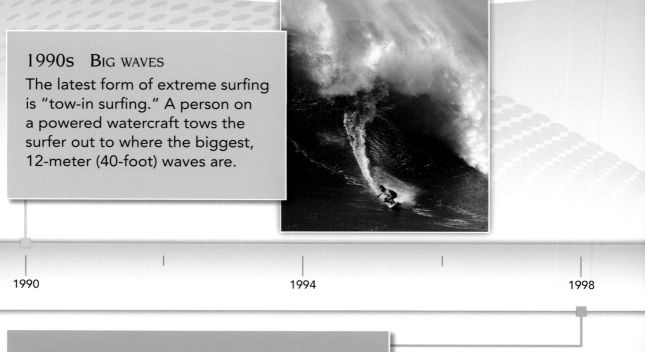

1990s BIG WAVES

The latest form of extreme surfing is "tow-in surfing." A person on a powered watercraft tows the surfer out to where the biggest, 12-meter (40-foot) waves are.

1990   1994   1998

1998

Snowboarding became a sport at the Winter Olympics in Japan. Olympic snowboarding is completed on a prepared course.

2004

Major League Baseball began to test players for banned drugs during the baseball season.

2007
U.S. basketball superstar LeBron James was at the top of the list of the world's richest under-25-year-olds. From 2006 to 2007 he earned $27 million.

2002   2006   2010

2008
At the Beijing Olympics in China, U.S. swimmer Michael Phelps won eight gold medals—the most anyone has won at an Olympic Games.

2008
The UEFA Champions League (soccer's European Cup) final in Russia was played between two British teams for the first time. Manchester United beat Chelsea in an exciting match.

Rising to the Challenge

Slow down, please!

Some people are fed-up with speed-driven sports, when life itself is so fast and tiring. Slow sports offer an alternative. The winner of a slow bicycle race is the person who takes the longest to finish the course!

The cyclist at the front is losing this slow bicycle race!

Athletes love their sports and will overcome all kinds of challenges to take part. Athletes also help others to overcome difficulties, too. Many sports events raise money for charities.

There is a lot of money to be made in sports, but you do not need much money to enjoy them. The most popular sport in the world to watch and play is soccer. To play it you only really need a cheap ball and some friends!

An inspiration

In 1998 U.S. racing cyclist Lance Armstrong returned to cycling after fighting cancer. He went on to win the Tour de France cycling competition seven times. He then retired for a while, but was back again in 2009. He races to raise money to help and to inspire people who have cancer.

Lance Armstrong (at the front) and his teammates cycle up the steep route of the Tour de France in 2009.

Key Dates

c. 3000 BCE
Ancient Egyptian pharaohs practice running to show off their god-like strength.

776 BCE
The first ancient Olympic Games are held in Olympia, Greece.

192 CE
Chariot racing is at its most popular in ancient Rome.

1325–1521
The Aztecs force their prisoners of war to play tlachtli. Teams compete to get a rubber ball through a stone ring.

1400s
Golf begins to be played in Scotland.

c. 1700
A popular form of **kung fu** develops in China, called wing chun (which means "eternal springtime").

1744
The rules for **cricket** are written down.

1845
The first U.S. baseball teams and clubs are formed.

1896
Crowds and athletes travel to the first modern Olympic Games, in Athens, Greece.

1940s
Around the world, **segregation** in sports is still common.

1958
About 45 million viewers watch the National Football League Championship Game on television.

1960
The Ethiopian runner Abebe Bikila runs barefoot to become the winner of the Olympic marathon.

1965
The first Pan-African Games are held in Congo.

1975
A match called the "Thrilla in Manila" takes place between U.S. heavyweight boxers Muhammad Ali and Joe Frazier.

1988
Canadian sprinter Ben Johnson is found guilty of taking drugs at the Olympics in Seoul, South Korea, and his gold medal is taken away.

1998
Snowboarding becomes a sport at the Winter Olympics in Japan.

2008
At the Beijing Olympics in China, U.S. swimmer Michael Phelps wins eight gold medals.

Glossary

advertising display of a product on television or on posters to help sell it

amateur someone who does a sport for a hobby, not a job. Amateur athletes do not get paid for their skills.

apartheid system of separating whites and non-whites in South Africa. Apartheid meant the non-whites were treated unfairly.

civilization particular society or culture at a particular period of time

cricket bat-and-ball sport begun in the United Kingdom. Baseball, which is similar, developed from cricket.

desegregation encouraging people to do everything together, no matter what their skin color is

engine machine that burns fuel to turn energy into movement

Industrial Revolution period from 1750 to 1850 when items started to be made in factories by machines

kung fu form of self-defense using kicks and punches. Kung fu is a martial art, similar to karate.

lacrosse game in which players catch a hard ball in a net on a stick

prehistoric before records were written down in any way

professional someone who does something as a job, not a hobby

racial prejudice belief that a person's skill or talent depends on that person's race

religious rite ceremony linked to religious beliefs. Many sports began as religious rites.

rugby game begun in the United Kingdom. Football developed from rugby, although rugby has some different rules, such as allowing players to kick and dribble the ball.

segregation separating people according to the color of their skin

slave servant who is not paid, but rather owned

spinal cord nerve cells in the backbone that connect much of the body to the brain. People with bad spinal cord injuries may not be able to walk.

sponsorship giving money to help someone do something

USSR Union of Soviet Socialist Republics, which later split into the Russian Federation and other countries

World Cup soccer tournament held every four years

Find Out More

Books

Bingham, Jane. *World History: Welcome to the Ancient Olympics!* Chicago: Raintree, 2008.

Great Teams series. Chicago: Raintree, 2006.

The Making of a Champion series. Chicago: Heinemann Library, 2005.

Middleton, Haydn. *The Olympics: Ancient Olympic Games*. Chicago: Heinemann Library, 2008.

Platt, Richard. *They Played What?!: The Weird History of Sports and Recreation*. Minnetonka, Minn.: Two-Can, 2007.

Websites

Learn more about the history of baseball at this website:

www.pbs.org/kenburns/baseball/

Learn more about the history of football at this website:

www.nfl.com/history

Find out about record-holders in a range of sports and games on the Guinness World Records website:

www.guinnessworldrecords.com/records/sports_and_games

Read more about the Ancient Olympics:

www.perseus.tufts.edu/Olympics/

Place to visit

The Exploratorium
3601 Lyon Street
San Francisco, California 94123
Tel: (415) 561-0360

Index